To
Ged Young
Kind Regards

Ingrid Loyau-Kennett

She was born in Orléans (45) in 1964 to a British mother (English and Scottish) and a Breton father. After a childhood in Picardy, and studies in Paris, she left to live in the United Kingdom with her two children. Despite studying history, the chances of life led her to become a modern language teacher in the United Kingdom and New Zealand.

Also by Ingrid Loyau-Kennett

"The Little Story of the Big Story" 1984
"A Study of the Dreyfus Affair through the Media" 1986
"The Fled (because the feminine is not a dirty word)" 2020

13 MINUTES

INGRID LOYAU-KENNETT

13 MINUTES

Author's note

Dear reader,

Let me thank you, first of all, for having bought my book. I sincerely hope you will enjoy it.

The title "13 Minutes" recalls the thirteen minutes I spent talking to Lee Rigby's killer Michael Adebolajo.

"13 Minutes" retraces as faithfully as possible what I experienced and what I thought, my impressions and my feelings, so that, when you read it, you feel as if you were me.

I don't use any names since I didn't know them at the time. I only describe the people present. Therefore when I write "a black man" or "a white woman" or even "a Caribbean woman", there is absolutely no racist prejudice at all what so ever, simply the description of a person that I cannot alter nor suppress as I have no other way to tell you about someone.
So it is with all the adjectives used in this book: there is no malice behind any of them. In these times, I wanted to make myself clear. And I thank you for understanding me.

Finally, this book establishes the real unfolding of these thirteen minutes, unfolding that we have already tried to change several times. I don't claim to have acted in such an extraordinary way that history should remember me, but I don't want my story to be changed.

With love

Ingrid

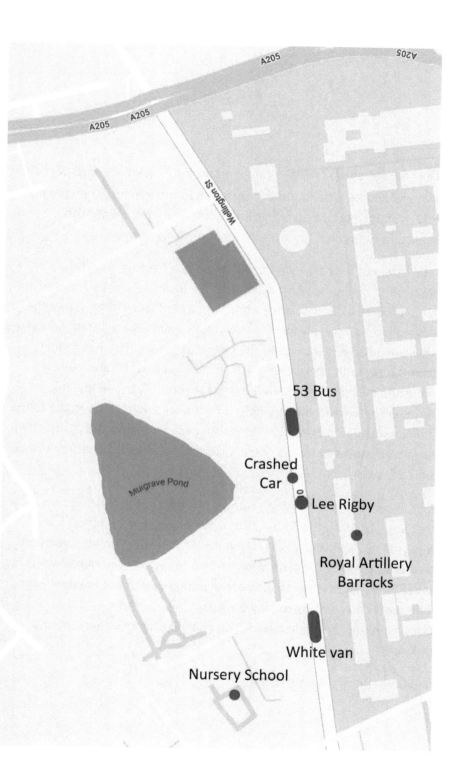

Prologue

Ten years already! Twelve exciting months during which I had never had so many people around me and taking an interest in me. Then the big void. Nothing. Returning to this loneliness never filled since the departure of my children who left to find work far away.

I still have not fully assimilated my status as a heroine, nor the description of courage heard about me by dear friends. This caused me some problems of conscience when I answered journalists, sometimes making me stammer. Now that everything seems like a distant memory, will I still be able to answer to the future questions that await me. I cannot talk about myself, let alone lie. Will I at least be able to talk about the events? It is not easy to repeat yourself, to see the images again and again. More worryingly, it no longer seems to be linked to the "official story", the one that the newspapers have reported in their own way and that the court has heard. After all, only I know what I saw and did. Let's see!

First, it seems that everything started two minutes before my arrival. At that time, I was on the 53 bus with a pile of luggage. I had just spent a week in France visiting my family and friends whom I do not see often, on the occasion of the profession of faith of my beloved nephew Jeremy. Seven stops, thousands of kilometres and several bags of sweets: sugar for energy and chewing to stay awake.
Ten days of joy and nightmare followed by five restful days with my children.

And then, these thirteen minutes…

Two Weeks Previously

For the first time, my journey begins badly. All my euros are stolen from me on the ferry. I still haven't figured out how. Fortunately, I have a few pounds left. "What an idea to take so much cash on you!" I hear myself say. The problem is that in France, the banks no longer keep cash because, I was told, of a long history of robberies. Banks therefore ensured that only their customers could use the ATMs. Long story short: no more way to withdraw money with a British Visa card in France, except in large cities, at the head office of banks which still keep a bit of money in their safe. So I am leaving with two-thirds of my savings changed to euros and one-third left in sterling just in case. And of course in a well serviced car, always done before long trips.

Well revised, that is what I thought. But this time, the mechanic had not done his job well. I was about to find out that the thermostat was faulty. So I am leaving almost without money and in a car that was going to die eight days later, but which for the moment was taking me to the southeast of France, to the Swiss border where my sister and her family live, via six other departments to go and hug my friends.

I had several reasons to take my car for such a long trip, despite the fatigue that such a journey would bring. First and foremost, my autonomy. Then, it had been so long since I had seen my youngest sister and her family that my niece made me promise to come with family photos. So I had half a dozen albums, a mountain of gifts not only for them but also for all my friends with who I would be visiting. Finally, I had made myself comfortable: the creasable clothes were hanging; the shoes were on the floor. I only had a small, light suitcase easy to lug around, with all the necessities for one night.

From Cornwall, where I am currently surviving, my first stop is London, to go and kiss my darling children. I take advantage of the car to bring them summer clothes and all those things which are cheaper in the provinces than in London, even though bought in the supermarkets of the same names.

Six days and four stops after my departure, my car is starting to overheat. I suspect a lack of water. So I add more but it doesn't help much. Not being in a hurry, I stop more often. I finally arrive near the hamlet where my sister lives. After a small panic at the sight of snow on the shoulders of the road (I hadn't planned the chains or studded tires in May), the anxiety mounts: there are no signposts to guide me to her hamlet. Moreover, apart from "Switzerland" and "the East", no town is signposted. I call my sister who, as usual, sends me on my way because she is busy and does not have time to pick me up. Fortunately, my niece and my sister's best friend present at her home at that time, took pity on me and came to meet me. As I have been driving in circles for twenty minutes before my rescue, my car has overheated. Fortunately, the day ends well around an aperitif (my favourite French tradition).

The next day, Jeremy's profession of Faith, everything goes well until the middle of the night. As usual, I wake up to go to the bathroom. As I try to get up, I realise I cannot feel my right leg anymore. So, I look at my foot in order to put it flat on the ground then I stand up. CRACK! Something in my ankle and one of the foot's small bone break. Despite the antalgics that I take to fight the pain of fibromyalgia, this pain is sharp and the ankle no longer responds. Not daring to jump on one foot, I miserably drag myself to the toilet. Still in shock from the sensation and cracking sound, I try to understand what could have happened. No doubt, one of the instep bones is broken. Not knowing what to do and, having forgotten my protective bandages for once, I go back to bed.

The next morning, I talk to my sister about it. She takes me to hospital. After waiting for two hours, I am finally seen. An X-ray confirms that one of the tendons has ruptured, breaking a small bone in the process, the why of the rupture remaining mysterious. The nurse wants to cast me but I refuse: I cannot drive with a heavy plaster cast. So she prescribes me a lightweight plastic cast that I can put on and take off as I please. I pick it up at the pharmacy.

The following day, I hit the road again. I have a long way to go, a heating car and a swollen ankle. Two hours later, I finally find a garage. I hope for a repair- he gives my car a death sentence. The thermostat no longer works. This is the reason for the motor overheating: the water can no longer do its duty as a cooler. The engine has overheated, there is nothing more to do. "Impossible!" The word is screaming in my head. I have a ferry in four day time, my ex, my uncle and my godfather to see, a car full of shopping and presents, a son whose birthday is in a few days and a damaged foot. Absolute nightmare!
"No choice", I say to my car with which I sometimes have little talks, "you have to hold on". I have to give up visiting my godfather in the Loiret and my uncle in Brittany because they live too far away. I change my reservation on the ferry and I bring forward my visit to my ex. I'm not cancelling it because I'm passing very close to his home to go up to Calais; I might as well stop there and rest the car.

I drive slowly. I use gallons of water to cool the engine. And miracle! I arrive at my children's father's, late but I'm there. Last stop of my trip, last friend to visit. I, very optimistically, try to reassure myself on the fact that if the engine has worked for more than eight hours today, well, after a good night's rest, there should not be any problem to cover the last three hours of the trip to the ferry. I drive slowly, I stop, I water. I don't worry about missing the ferry, there will always be another one. I just want my car to survive to the UK.

Unfortunately, she will never see England again. She decides to die near Saint-Quentin, a town full of friends, which saw me grow up, two hours from the ferry. I push my car to the side of the road and wait. I had opted to drive on an A road instead of the motorway just in case. This would make it easier to find help. The town is only a mile away but too far to walk with my ankle. My mobile phone died too- I have no way to call a friend. I have no more money. I have had it. It is hell! So I wait. I rely on the hand of God or my guardian angel. Provided that one of the two is aware of my troubles.

About an hour later, a City Services van pulls up. The driver asks me nicely if he can do anything he says I cannot stay here. I send him to negotiate this point with my car while I explain to his colleague that the car is dead and that I need help to go downtown to my best friend's. From there, it will be easier to organise the removal of the car and my repatriation. They agree to drop me and my luggage off at her house.

A forty year friendship is of course not a free pass on private life and I feel sorry for disturbing her, especially at lunchtime, in the middle of the lunch rush (she runs a small restaurant with her companion). I quickly explain the situation to her. With a smile, she hands me the keys over to her house. I pile up all my belongings in the guest room, release the two City employees after many thanks and I monopolise her telephone.

I find a scrap yard that will take care of my car and one of its employees will later pick me up from my friend's, on the way to my car. Then I organise my return: a ticket for the Eurostar (a small fortune) and one for the bus to take me there. Then, as if on purpose just to add more complication to an already stressful situation, it is impossible to book the bus on the internet; I have to go to the train station. Problem is they have never accepted a single payment from my English bank card. So I have to wait for my friend's return to see with her for a fund transfer from my bank account to hers, so that I can then pay for my bus trip with cash. Given the problems I have in France with my Visa card from Great Britain, I always organise a backup with my children before leaving. The French want the EU. But when it comes to putting it into practice, there is no one left. Foreign Visa cards are accepted in all stores but there is no way to withdraw cash, pay for the motorway or buy a train ticket in France.

When the employee of the scrapyard insistently asks me for the French Carte Grise of the car, I try to give him the British equivalent, the car's green card, a card which indicates the name of the owner of the car and assorted to the car's technical sheet, in one word, a green Carte Grise somehow. But he does not want it. He insisted for a French one. "Look dude, my car is English. Can't have French paperwork!" I want to shout at him. Instead, I quietly explain to him that it does not matter anyway because now, in EU, cars' papers are no longer required. "Don't know" he replied.

Too tired with a tormenting ankle and foot, I leave the car to him until he is willing to learn how the EU works and how a lot of procedures are now much simpler. I ask him to inquire about them and to come back to me at my friend's when he's done in order to complete the car' end of life paperwork. To this day, I am still waiting. In fact, the car had a new battery, two new tires, and a full tank of gas that he had offered to buy back from me. Instead, he has kept everything, never to contact me again.

A little annoyed to have an extra chore in her busy schedule, my friend Chrystelle still goes to the ATM to take the money I need and paid into her account by my daughter. She especially struggles to understand why my Visa card is hardly accepted in France considering the UK is part of the European Union.
I can finally buy my bus ticket which will take me to this Eurostar station lost in the middle of a field, without any town or village around, nicknamed by the people of the North "the Daisy station". Last chore: to pack up as many things as possible, leaving in my friend's care what I can't take for lack of extra hands. Chrystelle kindly invites me to spend the night at her house, and it is around an aperitif that we prepare dinner. For the first time of the day, I can rest and above all free my ankle from my weight.

Pawony, my daughter, is very impatient to see me arrive. We are very, very close. Since the theft of my euros, she has begun to worry. Needless to say what state she is in right now. Since my ankle and foot injuries, she calls me ten times a day, asking me what she can do. When I am reluctant to take the Eurostar because of the cost, she insists I do, telling me that money does not matter, the main thing being that I get there as soon as possible, so that I can rest and she can take care of the rest. Bless her! My son Basil, as close to me as his sister is, also worries sick. But he doesn't know what to say or what to do. Bless him! It is true that I can't wait to be back, to feel safe in my country and with my children who love me as much as I love them.

May 22. Four days have gone; four days of rest, pampered by my daughter and cuddled by my son, very relieved to see me in one piece. We celebrated Basil's 23rd birthday on the 19th. The only fly in the ointment was the local hospital's refusal to cast or support my ankle in any way, as the nurse decided after looking at the x-ray that my ankle was fine. Ah! These nurses who think they are doctors! Never mind! said my daughter who went to buy bandages and did it herself. She is so sweet!

May 22, then. Today I am going home. FINALLY! This trip had cost me a fortune, my best shoes (as the bus driver has lost them) and my independence as I live in a rural area with very little public transport. My children left that morning, one for work, the other one to look for a job. I shall meet them later at Victoria Station. I am alone.

The coach for Cornwall does not leave until late in the afternoon; I have plenty of time to get ready and go to Parliament Square on the 53 bus. I take a bath. I have dinner (lunch). Then, around 1.50 p.m, I go out to catch my bus. Suddenly, as the bus approaches, I realise that I forgot my phone charger. I go back to get it and I miss the bus. I shall be off to take the next one. Fate does not matter much.
It is past 2.00 p.m. when I get on the next bus with my mountain of luggage. Being at the start of the line, I am able to sit comfortably .

I like to take the bus, and visit London at the same time. It really is a very beautiful city. Lost in thought, reliving those horrible ten days, I do not immediately process that the bus has stopped. Through the window, I look around and see what looks like an accident. A car has crashed against a lamppost. A man of African origin paces back and forth nervously; a man is lying in the middle of the street; a woman of Caribbean origin caresses his back. I remember having seen in a documentary that this was the way the Caribbean people take care of the dead, even those they do not know. So I understand what she is doing. Finally, I look at the traffic condition to check if the street has been blocked. By avoiding traffic jams, emergency services can access victims more easily. My bus stands on one side of the street; a white van blocks the opposite side. There is nobody. I imagine the accident just happened. In fact, I will discover later that two minutes had already passed.

What this Caribbean lady is doing is very commendable and full of love, but I tell myself that it will not save the victim's life while waiting for help. I ask the driver to get out of the bus in order to provide first aid to this injured person. I do not know what awaits me.

First minute

The door opens, I get out of the bus. I look around me, counting the curious bystanders as an approximate indication as to when the accident took place. In a medium-traffic street, around ten onlookers stop per minute. There, except for the manager or employee of the small store who talks with the driver of the white truck, there is nobody. The truck is blocking the traffic on its side. No car behind. Did the accident just happen?

I walk towards the victim without paying attention to the black man. Given his nervousness, he must be the driver of the wrecked car. He is certainly thinking about the consequences of his inattention or perhaps trying to understand what happened. He does not look hurt. He does not interest me. The victim first. When I see the condition of the car, I expect the worst: bone fractures with maybe an open fracture on one of the legs, which means haemorrhage, head trauma, internal bleeding... I find worrying that he does not move. He must have lost conscienceless. I hope the ambulance arrives quickly. I imagine that the emergency services have been notified. I think of what to do, the four steps of First Aid: Assess, Plan, Implement, Evaluate. If I have to apply pressure to stop the bleeding, I will not be able to put him in the recovery position. And even if I could, would that be reasonable? He was rammed at high speed from what I can deduce by seeing the car crushed into the lamppost all the way to the windshield. The best option would be to take care of stopping the flow of blood and clearing the airways rather than moving him.

As I walk towards the victim, I think back to all those road accidents I have witnessed in my life. Today, there are far fewer. But twenty years ago and more, I saw one every two years on average, even more some years. I do not remember all of them, but the first one still really stands out to me, an accident looking similar to this one. I still remember it to this day.

I was just 18 years old, I had just joined the Scouts de France after a whole life spent with the Guides de France: a desire for change, a desire to be with boys. To become a leader, you have to learn a number of skills, among other things: first aid gestures. It was less than two weeks since I had just been certified as a First Aider by the Red Cross when a traffic accident happened in front of me.

I was walking on the pavement, rue de Rennes in Paris, looking for the store that sold the study books I needed when suddenly, a car drove up the pavement at high speed, hitting a young man who was walking in front of me. I immediately went to his aid while asking passers-by who were beginning to crowd around him to watch, to call for help. I bent over the victim who had fallen on his back and realised he was bleeding from the head, but mostly from the ears and mouth. I had learned that this could be a sign of internal bleeding. Immediately, with my fists, I opted to compress the arteries on the upper thighs to slow the blood flow rather than placing him in the safety position. But I had to stop because the driver, a young female, kept screaming. So I got up to go to her car. The Red Cross had taught us that the only way to calm someone in this hysterical state was to slap them (this happened in 1982). My whole body was trembling. Knowing that I could probably do this only once, I took a deep breath and slapped her. Rightly enough, it calmed her down instantly. I then turned back to the young man who was moaning ominously.

Not sure he could hear me, I talked to him while compressing his arteries. I asked him his name but he did not answer me. The bleeding had stopped; I was happy to see that my pressures were the right thing to do because at this stage, I was not sure of anything. After all, it was my first case, the first time I intervened as a First Aider. I have never been so glad to hear the ambulance siren. I did not know why I was shivering so

*much because I was not afraid and, on this beautiful sunny day, I was
not cold.*

*Two paramedics approached the young man and me. I was about to get
up when a paramedic asked me to stay and continue. He also asked me
what had happened. I described to him how the young man was thrown
into the air and then fell on his back and head. It was because he had
fallen on his back that I hadn't dared to put him in the recovery position.
In addition, I thought it was better to do pressures on his arteries
because I suspected internal bleeding. He was moaning a lot in a
worrying way and I could not get him to say his name. Worried, I looked
at the paramedic and asked him if I had done the right thing. He
reassured me and replied that I had probably saved this man's life.*

*Then he left and returned a minute later with some equipment. He took
over and I was finally able to get up. I was shaking so much that I had
trouble standing up. Suddenly, fatigue overtook me. The paramedic
looked at me and invited me to stay in the second ambulance because,
he told me, I was very pale, so I did.*

*Inside the ambulance, I was given a glass of water and a few drops of
tonic on a sugar lump. I could not help but think that paramedics in the
twentieth century still have the same treatments as my nineteenth
century great-grandmother. I was invited to stay as long as my body
needed to assimilate all that adrenaline, which was the cause of my
shaking.*

Twenty minutes later, I resumed the course of my life.

Here I am near the victim. From his clothes and shoes, he appears to be
a young man. His head is covered by his jacket. Blood is flowing on the
street coming out of his head or around. He is bleeding: he is therefore
alive. In any case, his heart beats. I kneel down to grab his wrist to find
his pulse. I do not feel anything. The Caribbean woman tells me he is
dead. I tell her that he is bleeding so his heart may be beating. Then, not
being able to feel his pulse on his wrist, I begin to lift the jacket to find it

on the jugular artery, under the jaw and, in the process, try to assess his injuries in order to bring him the necessary help before the arrival of the ambulance. The Caribbean woman, while stroking his back, repeats to me that he is dead. (I learned from the papers that her name is Amanda Donnelli)

Suddenly, I hear a man's voice ordering me not to approach my hand closer (to the neck), not to touch the body. Still kneeling, I pivot on my feet to the right, towards the voice and my gaze fell on two bloody hands, one holding a gun, the other one a butcher's cleaver and a large sharp knife. Only the cleaver is covered in blood. This is when I tell myself that something is wrong. This does not look like a road crash. My fondness for detective stories makes me suspect that it is a murder.

So, while getting up, I look at the pavement behind the man, over his shoulder, to see any clues as to indicate if this man could have killed this young man. I see that at the beginning of the sidewalk, there is no barrier and therefore a car can drive on it. Then, looking up along it, I see a big splatter of blood. It is undoubtedly there that the young man was struck. Then, from the splash, I see two streaks of blood. This man with the bloody hands, for some reason, dragged his victim to the middle of the street. It is not an accident. This young man has been killed.

Second minute

I am now standing, facing a tall, very black man, obviously of African origin. He is tall but a little less than me, so I lower myself a bit so as to not outsize him and I put my hands in my coat pockets to appear unfrightening . Avoiding his gaze, I stare at him and inspect him. He does not seem to be mental, neither drunk nor on drugs.

"Why?" I ask him, questioning him about his ban on approaching the body

"Because I just killed him".

"Why?"

"Because he is a British soldier and he kills Muslim civilians in Islamic countries".

"Ah!" I replied, a little dubious. Nothing in the young man's clothing betrays his status as a soldier. I am not convinced at all by his explanation.

Suddenly, it hits me. This man whom I have seen nervously pacing and whom I had assumed was the driver of the vehicle and responsible for the accident, is in fact not nervous: he is frustrated. Frustrated because he has committed an abominable act and no one is there to see it. Was he pacing, wondering if he has to commit another murder to finally get the attention he is looking for? To relieve him of any desire to start over, I start talking to him while waiting for the police to arrive. From the bus, I think I have noticed a police station on the other side of the boulevard. So I expect they are going to arrive very quickly. As usual, when it comes to public services, I am wrong.

[I will learn later that just after his heinous act, he had forced a passer-by to film on their smart phone a hate message explaining his action; that when I got off the 53 bus, the crime had not just happened as I had thought when I saw no onlookers around, but had taken place two to three minutes earlier (Weird this absence of onlookers); that three cars each containing a couple passed by the scene of the accident before the beheading of the young man, before the white truck stopped and none of them went to help the victim. They did not even block the street as the Highway Code commands to do. Shame on them!]

His explanation does not hold water. First of all because, this African man speaks an excellent English with a perfect London accent, which is quite surprising because black people, especially Africans, often have a more or less pronounced accent, a way of speaking that is personal to them, a cultural identity. So he received an excellent education.
Then, he does not look like a Muslim because their religion dictates them to wear a beard and he is beardless.
I try to quickly come up with ideas. I do not want to leave any time out; I do not want him to go back to his killing ideas. I caught his attention and I want to keep it.

I look around me. A few people have stopped and are staring at us.
Then, I notice much further up to the left, a young black man leaning against a railing. He does not look in our direction; He is not moving; he does not seem to be a bystander. Maybe is he waiting for someone?
I still do not hear any police nor ambulance sirens.

Suddenly, a young black girl tumbles, passing between the killer and me and shout to her mother: "Come on mum, let him and come shopping". Come shopping? The situation is serious; a man has just been seriously injured and all she thinks about is shopping. I understand very well that a setback can be unfortunate, but there are limits to indecency.

Her mother shakes her head. So she retreats very unhappy.
Her mother is this Caribbean lady. She is still there, sitting on the ground and still stroking the victim's back. She says nothing; she seems to be

praying in her head. I wonder what she is really thinking to herself as she caresses the dead man's back. The documentary did not specify this point. Are there ready-made prayers that are recited as Catholics say their rosary? Or do they improvise? Do they address a god or the ancestors? The culture of different peoples of the Earth has always fascinated me. This diversity is beautiful and constitutes a richness that globalisation and a few big brands are trying to destroy by standardising the planet. This Caribbean woman, while living in England, remains Caribbean even in front of a European dead. I find her beautiful.

The killer leaves me to meet the other black man, the one leaning against a gate. The latter comes to meet him, limply. The killer hands him the long pointy knife and then comes back to me. The other returns to the gate. I don't think they spoke to one another. It was quick. The penny drops: they are together, partners in crime, literally.

The killer seems to be waiting for my questions. He calmed down a lot; he is more relaxed, literally like a rubber band pulled so hard it was ready to snap and now would give slack. His voice is calm, peaceful. Although it is not a social conversation, he seems to appreciate my presence and my interest in him.

So much the better because I am not sure what I am doing. I had come to help a wounded man; I find myself talking to a killer. Not for a second, the idea that he could be a terrorist came to my mind. He was just a man with a stupid idea to kill another one for some even more stupid reason I did not believe. Why did the urge to talk to him arise instead of returning to the bus where all my luggage is waiting for me? Why do I want to calm him down, perhaps prevent him from killing again? Why do I want to help the police, who at home in Cornwall, refuse to arrest those who verbally or physically assault me or vandalise my house? In fact, it all came together. I did not premeditate anything. Every second is improvised, based on the killer's reactions and responses. I do not know how it will end; anyway I do not think of it.

The pain from my damaged ankle and the little broken bone remind me of my own predicament. Thinking I would be sitting for several hours, I did not put on my ankle brace, preferring to let the blood flow. My ankle and my foot are therefore not protected and I am standing there talking to him playing the decompression valves.

Like a dog sniffing the air looking for its prey, I listen for the slightest sound that would tell me if help is on the way. Still nothing.

Third minute

Although I saw him approach the other man, and he cannot help but suspect that I saw them, I do not tell him. Something in my head tells me to ignore his action and therefore, not ask the killer any questions about his accomplice.

As I am about to continue talking to him, I see a middle-aged white European woman approaching. I see her looking at me, looking at the killer and his hands. Then, she goes nearer the victim and examines him. I am outraged. I want to shout in her face that we're not at the circus, that it's not a show, and that she could have some respect for the victim. I am mostly worried about the killer's reaction.

"While you are at it, take some pictures," I tell her sarcastically.

She looks at me again then leaves. Without a word. I cannot believe it. To stop in order to watch an accident, to wallow in the misery of others, is shocking enough. But there. Personally, I can't stand it.

It reminds me of the movies with *Charlot* by Charlie Chaplin or Laurel and Hardy's. There is always someone to whom a thousand unpleasant things happen, just to make us laugh. I never found it funny. How can one watch someone fall from a ladder, get hurt, get a bucket over their head, get covered in paint or cement, or even fall into an icy river and laugh? How can one laugh watching Hardy slap Laurel? I always exclaim, "Oh! Poor guy!" I pity the one to whom all misery befalls, the one who is the other's Turkish head.

The Table Turns on the Gardener, everyone laughs. I run in with a towel. I am usually the only one who does it. It must be ridiculous but I cannot help it. Being wet is not funny, and instead of laughing, I feel as cold as the wet person. I am like that. I cannot stand these people who watch, those who stand there and stare at smashed cars and drivers in shock or watch the injured bleed or cry out in pain. I cannot stand that they do nothing and even less if they dare comment. I understand the distresses of the situation. I try to comfort the victims as best as I can. And if possible, I am trying to save a life. I cannot do much because I am not a doctor but I give what I have: attention, time, comfort, because in these painful moments, a little can be huge and make such a difference.

I let him continue to explain to me that this crime is revenge, avenging the innocent victims of British soldiers. I ask him what he is trying to achieve. After all, he just killed someone and since he seems smart and in full control, he did it for a reason. He wants something. He talks about revenge but killing someone like this is not very explicit for an ordinary mortal.

"I want to kill English soldiers to avenge the Muslim women and children they kill," he repeats to me while giving me some additional details.

"Ah!" I answer. Yet I haven't heard anything like it on the news. "Are you sure?"

"Yes."

"Killing a soldier will not have much an impact. What do you want?"

"War!"

"Oh. Where? In England?" I ask him

"Yes."

"Here in the streets of London?"

"Yes," he answers me

"You're going to lose. It's only you versus all of us."

"I do not care!"

"Ah!"

I do not really know what to answer to that. It makes me think of that time when I was unable to answer my children after a serious incident, an incident caused by a drunkard, who, with a frontal collision, had killed an old man who was coming from the opposite direction.

We had been living in New Zealand for a few years already and I worked a lot, teaching French, English and history by day and translator by night for an Australian company. I had just finished giving my English lessons to Koreans who employed me privately after poaching me from the language school where I worked.

I was going home around 10 p.m. when a car refused me the right of way. It was in Auckland.   In New Zealand, driving is on the left hand-side and right-turning cars have priority; cars in the opposite direction turning left, so left to left, must stop. Contrary to what is practiced in Europe Thus, by blocking the traffic, they secure the cars which, when turning right, must cross the street and pass in front of them. As this priority is unique in the world, anyone who did not grow up in New Zealand often forgets it. I personally had to make an effort to concentrate every time I got behind the wheel so as not to forget this particular priority.

That is how I saw this car cut me off. Then the traffic intensifying, I had to wait several minutes before being able to enter the street on the right. Shortly after, I saw something like a crowd around two cars blocking the road. I recognised the car that had refused me priority, crashed by a car coming in the opposite direction. The shock was frontal. I could see the driver who had caused the accident was not the one who had cut me off. He had got out of his car as well as his friend and they seemed to be doing well. On the other hand, there was no movement coming from the other car. So I parked and got out of my car to check on the other driver's health. He was a man of at least seventy years old and rather chubby. He was cold. He had no pulse. He was dead. He had no injuries: his car had well withstood the impact. I therefore concluded that he had had a heart attack certainly due to the shock of the accident and that no cardiac massage could resuscitate him. So, I walked over to the other driver who was getting noisy. He was obviously inebriated. He accused the other driver of being in his way, that is to say on the right side of the street since the alcoholic had driven on the wrong side; of having damaged his new car; and prevented him from speeding to show his male friend how fast his car was. He was insulting the man, the victim. I silenced him by revealing to him that this man was dead, that he had killed him out of selfishness and recklessness. As his friend backed away in shame, I also shot him a few words, reproaching him for not having prevented his friend from driving and mistaking the streets of the city for a racing circuit; that he was as much responsible for the death of the other driver as his "buddy". Then someone came to tell me that the police were coming. Tired from a long day of work, and no life endangered by injuries, I decided to leave before the arrival of help, but not before having taken note of his license plate, registration and make of his car, just in case.

Consequently, I arrived home a little later than usual. I explained to my children what had just happened in a light tone, the story of an idiot who should have never been granted a driver's license, one of those immature young men who thinks they can do everything they wish regardless of the consequences to others, including driving after drinking and speeding on the streets.
Suddenly, I saw my children on the verge of tears. Surprised, I asked them what was going on. One of them answered me: "Mum, do you realise that it is you who could have been killed if this old man had not cut you off? What would we have done without you?" Shock! I had not realised I should have been the accident victim. I admitted I hadn't thought about it, then I felt my stomach knot. I did not know what to answer them. I suddenly did not feel well. So we hugged for a long time and everything was fine.

The following days, each time I got behind the wheel, their question bothered me. If I had arrived three seconds earlier, the old man would not have cut me off. And if I had been killed, what would have happened to my children? It is great to live in New Zealand but all of our family lives in Europe and Asia. We were alone there and all the money we had was the one I earned. My children were grown but still under age; therefore, they could not have done anything without parental representation. And without money. I could not find any answer to this problem but I doubled up my attention when driving.

Fourth minute

I talk to him normally but I leave time between each sentence. It is not in my habits but I do not know how he will react to my words. Moreover, mentally, I weigh each of my words: I do not want to express the idea that I approve of his action since I strongly condemn it, at the same time, I do not want to upset him by seeming to judge him. So far it works. He answers me without getting angry, although his short answers may mean that he does not want to talk. Surprisingly, he has not sworn at all. Not once did he use the 'F... word', the most vulgar word in the English language and too often heard in the mouths of young people as a way of giving themselves importance or to cover up a lack in language . This killer is really disconcerting, full of contrast. His speaking is the opposite of his action. Yet he brutally murdered a man. There must be a reason. For the moment, he speaks to me; he tolerates my presence, my interaction with him.

"Anyway, the police will be here soon and arrest you" I say, resuming the "conversation"

"I'll kill them."

"They will kill you."

"Good!" he concludes.

A suicide! He wants to be suicided. Is it because he does not have the courage to do it himself? Unless he wants to let the whole world know: "This is the shitty life you gave me. I don't want it. So you're going to kill me because I don't want to die alone in my corner and I want you to know." Perhaps, more simply, he does not want to end his life in prison. I look at the revolver he holds in his left hand. Although it looks real, somehow, I tell myself that it does not work. The reason behind having one is simple: pointing a gun at a cop is definitely the best way to get shot.

And the other one, does he want to be shot too? Is he aware of his accomplice's intentions? It cannot be said that the brutal attack on this poor young man has any effect on him. Nothing, no nervous reaction, no worries. He has as much energy as a statue as the killer has from a boosted battery. I wonder what he is doing here. What could have been his role in this savage aggression? A dog who followed his master?

Suddenly, in the distance, I hear sirens. The first since I arrived. I'm not sure which sirens it is: firemen, police, ambulance, I get them all mixed up. Anyway, they seem to sound from too far away to come here and all too quickly I no longer hear them. So it is not the help I am looking for. But what are they doing? I quickly glance an eye at the victim: the young man continues to bleed. It breaks my heart to not be able to do anything and to see that he is going to die on the street for lack of an ambulance arriving in time. Although, in the state he must be in, surviving might not be a gift.

I know that personally I would rather die than live a vegetable life because my brain would have been damaged, or lie on a bed paralysed in all four limbs and hooked up to an breathing machine because I cannot do it myself. What a daily nightmare!

When I see mentally handicapped people whom the medical world has declared to have no connection with this world, I hear frustration in their cry. Somehow they know what the others do and they cannot; how others are and what they are not. I am convinced that they perceive their surroundings with accuracy and that they can compare it with themselves. As they have never known anything else, they can more or less handle it. But I who have known the freedom of body and mind, would find it intolerable to be confined in my body. And you will never make me believe that a person who has gone into their own world does not perceive the one in which they live. Body and mind's imprisonment are worse than pain. I don't wish that on anyone.

It should be possible in certain cases, for those who so wish, to be able to choose to die rather than to remain alive, especially in the case of mental and physical paralysis and incurable diseases. Why spend so much money administering to an irremediably sick body? You have to die one day; you have to die of something. In my opinion based on the fact that it is more logical and "human", it is better to die well by choosing the moment of your death rather than to drag on in a deplorable situation and die miserably. I am told it is called euthanasia. I prefer the expression "Free to choose your own death".

But surely this young man has a mother who would like to keep him alive. And maybe he is not that hurt. So I pray that the ambulance comes, treats him and takes him to hospital. But what are they doing?

I am abruptly interrupted in my prayers by the daughter of this admirable Caribbean woman, who was still caressing the young man's back. What exactly is she doing, I cannot say. But it is a tender gesture that she gives him.

"So mum, are you coming to do this shopping? Leave him!" she shouts to her mother after having again passed between the killer and me. Her again! It is unbelievable to be so egocentric, so detached from the surrounding cruelty. This time, her mother gets up and talks to her, then she sits down. The girl leaves.

As she comes from behind me, I do not see her approaching and therefore, each time, she surprises me. I have to change position because if she still dares to come back, I want to stop her and slap her, to explain to her that we are in a serious and delicate situation; that his attitude can only aggravate the mood of the killer; that she might have some respect for the victim; and finally, that she has nothing to do here so she should leave and not come back. Her attitude is hard to believe.

But what is on her mind? I refuse to put all young people in the same basket but it is true that education, this so-called positive education, has greatly declined in quality and respect, whether it is that of the school or that of the parents.

Fifth minute

From time to time, I take a look around me, furtive, quick. I would like to know what is happening near us, but I dare not turn myself around. I do not want the killer to think my attention is not fully devoted to him. I am also a little afraid to know. Fear is not the exact word, rather anxiety. Anxious that maybe a few people have stopped and are staring at me, trying to hear what I'm saying to the killer.

I am positioned in such a way that I have my back to the part of the street adjacent to the boulevard and to the bus, more or less facing the white truck and the gate, therefore a fairly small space. So, not willing to turn around, I don't know what's going on behind me. The killer and I are alone in the middle of the street. Since everything is quiet, (I can barely hear three or four people speaking quietly), I really think we are alone with only the victim and the Caribbean woman close to us.

I surf on his idea of revenge:
"You know, civilian casualties are a fact of war, something that cannot be avoided. The enemy does not kill civilians on purpose. These deaths are only the collateral result of a battle. During World War II, the Luftwaffe bombarded London for several weeks with the aim of destroying the city. We called it the Blitz. Thousands of civilians were killed but that was not the goal; they were only collateral victims. It was war."

For the first time, he looks at me in the eye. He is stunned and says more to himself than me: "Really?" He looks genuinely surprised.
The teacher I was suddenly had this thought: What are they learning at school these days?

I was a teacher for almost twenty years and I know that the British school curriculum was not very extensive when my children were in primary school. Then the Labour party came to power and Tony Blair and his team decided that learning was traumatic. Therefore, they reduced the school curriculum even further. Today, the majority of public school students enter secondary school without knowing how to read or write. And history and geography are hardly taught. This man is young enough to have received this minimum education.

I, personally, have never accepted that my students remain ignorant. I often took the risk of not respecting the teaching policies given to teachers in Great Britain, such as the overall method for learning how to read. It is a nameless absurdity that produces illiterates. In my elementary classes, I always taught reading using the alphabetical method. In three months, all my pupils knew how to read and therefore write, and above all to appreciate school: when you understand a math problem because you know how to read the words and therefore you understand all of them, you know you have a chance to solve the problem. Consequently, the class hours become happier.

Nor have I ever agreed to lie to them: when an exercise was failed, I never said: "Bravo, that's good" (positive education) but "I see that you haven't understood, let me explain it to you."

I could clearly see that the student knew that they had not succeeded in finding the solution because they had not understood how to do it. To tell the student otherwise would have been an insult to their intelligence. It would also make the student doubt me since I was lying to them, me the adult whose role was to teach my students true things. At the same time, it undermined the trust that was established between us and essential to a good relationship, the good balance of the student and the success of their schooling. Had the killer suffered from this situation at school?

I did not talk to the killer about the civilian victims of a conflict to show him the pointlessness of his gesture, but because it upsets me. I am kind of naive. How can I say this? Though I am not convinced of his story, I believe that he believes it so I believe him. I do not know if I make myself understand. I just think if he had learned more about history at school, especially World War II in England, this young man, lying there on the ground in the middle of the street, might still be alive; that the killer would have found another way to declare his hatred of the society to the whole planet. This young man would have not been the innocent victim of an absurd revenge because it cannot have any impact on world events.

"If you want to kill British soldiers, why don't you join a regular army from a Muslim country? At least you could legally kill all the soldiers you want" I asked him to keep his attention.

"It's a good idea," he replies, "I hadn't thought of that."

Really? I thought. When one wants to kill soldiers, it is however the most logical action. Could the risk of getting hurt be too great for him? Unless the big idea is not to avenge innocent Muslim victims but for some obscure reason, to set up this incredible scenario from scratch. I cannot understand why I have such a hard time believing it. But there is no way I'll ask him. That would definitely piss him off and I don't care anyway. I want the police to come and arrest them both with no more deaths under their belt in order for the bus to resume my journey to Parliament Square. So, while waiting for the "police forces", I play his game. My right foot does not agree.

When my interlocutor is lying to me, I know it immediately. I quickly detect lies (slower if my interlocutor is a friend who generally does not lie to me). And it is reflected in my answers. They become naive and are first-degree answers. Therefore, the lie stops quickly when my interlocutor realises that it does not take with me. The killer continues. So I hesitate: is he lying to me or not? I do not think so. Is he lying to himself? Certainly. I am not trying to find out the reasons for his act;

they are indifferent to me. But knowing what is on his mind helps me talk to him without risk of upsetting him, helps me to agree with him without endorsing his murder (I do not think he would believe me if I was going along with it. He knows well that no sane person can condone his crime. I respect his intelligence). I have to keep his attention at all costs, divert his thoughts: that's all that matters for the moment.

Sixth minute

Then, for no particular reason, perhaps trying to keep a countenance during our silence, or maybe the idea of joining a regular Islamic army reminded him what he is holding in his hand, he begins to brandish his revolver.

I look at it then asks him, taking care not to name the object:
"It's real?

"Yes it's a real one," he replies.

"And it works?"

"Yes, in working order."

I'm sure not. I cannot say why but it reminds me more of a toy, one of those life-size metal revolvers sold with the cowboy costume. Anyway, he is not going to tell me it is not in working order if that is the case.

Having never been so close to a revolver, I have a strong desire to take it in my hand, to hold the stock tightly, to handle it, that is to say, to open the cylinder, to lower the barrel, engage the hammer and squeeze the trigger, like in the movies. Of course, in this context, it is out of the question to make such a request. Shame!

Months later, one evening, as I recalled the scene trying to understand my lack of reaction to a possibly loaded revolver, it occurred to me why I was so convinced the revolver posed no danger: if it had been in good working condition, the killer would have shot his victim rather than complicate matters with a car and knives. So it was just a prop, probably meant to make him visually more dangerous than he actually was. Besides, I will later learn that the gun was real but out of action.

It is amazing the work of the subconscious. My subconscious had analysed the situation and indicated to my conscious self the result of this analysis. We call it instinct. I called it "trusting yourself" which is not trying to understand why you want to do this or need to do that. My subconscious worked a lot during these thirteen minutes and for once, my consciousness listened very well. Hence this impression of courage I delivered when in fact, having no reason to be afraid, I was able to give the killer the attention he demanded for his crime. Regarding the revolver, I risked nothing. (This is, rightly or wrongly, what I thought).

"Really, it works?" I ask once again, with admiration in my voice, like 'Whoaaa! You've got a real gun. That's cool!'

"Yes," he answers me with, in a tone intended to convince me.

Then, he brings the weapon back along his leg. By this, I understand that he prefers we forget the gun and we start talking about something else. From time to time, he glances in the direction of his accomplice. He must verify that he is always there, waiting like him.

That is to say, what is he waiting for? I understand that he wants to attack and kill the police in order to get killed, but since no one is coming... It is obvious that his plan is very likely not to be executed the way he had planned. As long as the police are not present, there are more risks for the plan to be fanned. So why not run away? Considering the snail pace of the police force to handle the situation, he has time to cross all of London on foot without being worried. And even kill again. This is moreover what I dread the most.

Although he is fidgeting, he has calmed down a lot and the little he says, he says it without raising his voice, without getting angry and without swearing. His features are posed. His eyes only are very active, looking right, left, recording everything that happens. But, is it the calm before the storm? If he shows no anger, rage or hatred, not in his words nor in his post-murder actions, anxiety must begin to overwhelm him. After committing his crime, he chose to wait for the police to serve as their target. But as he is not seeing them coming, he must be starting to ask himself questions. In the meantime, anything can happen: someone wanting to avenge the young man, an Islamist passing by and wishing to join them... Anything is really possible.

I dare not broach the subject. If this slowness annoys him, he risks losing his temper. And although he seems to be respecting the female sex, an uncontrollable fit of rage can fuse. When one comes to act as he did, we have everything to fear. So I must relentlessly be on my guards.

With the creation of gun powder and bullets, then of revolvers, rifles and others firearms safer and easier to handle than their ancestors, killing is within reach of all, provided you know how to aim of course. No more having to stand at an arm length of the future victim or the enemy, of having to face their rage and their gaze, we can kill while standing ten or a hundred yards away. He stuck a knife in the body of a man. It does not seem much but it is not that easy. That requires a certain mind. This man is therefore to be feared despite his apparent calm. You should never underestimate people and situations if you want to avoid disasters.

Seventh minute

I therefore do not underestimate his possible reactions. He killed, he can do it again.

Revenge is all he has in mind. He says Muslim women and children are being killed by British soldiers. He just killed a soldier out of revenge, and now he wants to take on law enforcement. Fortunately, he does not seem to want to kill a non-Muslim woman or child. He does not talk about it. This Caribbean lady, who arrived there first, approached him to approach the victim and he did not react negatively, as far as I can see. Although I cannot tell if it is because this lady is black or simply a woman. Did she ask permission to "watch over" the victim or did she simply sit near the young man?

I am still relieved to know the kids are in school.

I keep talking to him:

"It is always possible for a man of goodwill to join a country's army, even if that man is not from that country. It is even easier for a Muslim to enlist in the army of an Islamic country. And the more disbelievers (non-Muslims) you kill, the more a feted and celebrated hero you become."

I am also very fond of documentaries: what happens elsewhere, the lives of others, how do we make this or that etc.... Everything fascinates me, arouses my curiosity and I like to learn and be knowledgeable. It therefore seems to me that from the depths of my brain, what I have just told him is true, a vague memory of documentaries from which I have preserved these snippets of information, in addition to having married the son of a Muslim lady, and consequently, to have learned at her contact.

It is important because not knowing how to lie (medically, it is called "lack of social imagination"), everything I say must be based on facts for me to be able to speak about them, realities which, in my head, are in the form of films or pictures. I am glad I know enough to talk to the killer. As the Scouts' motto proclaims: "Always Be Prepared".

In telling him this, I have the vague hope that if he would ever be free again, he will leave the UK to continue his revenge elsewhere since his thing is military related, unlike other terrorists who plant bombs everywhere to kill as many as possible disbelievers: men, women and children without distinction.

In Great Britain, a murder or an assassination is, generally, heavily punished by life imprisonment although one can never know when it is a jury that makes the final decision. And sentences are very often served in full. Reduced sentences are rare and amnesties non-existent. Also, if ever, a criminal sentenced to life should be released for compassionate reasons, usually to treat an incurable disease and die at home, he would spend the rest of his life "under license" in the community.

But I grew up in France where life means twenty years, if that, if the guy is unlucky, and twenty years, eight; where for a murder, the sentence is usually two years suspended because dozens of excuses are invoked to condemn lightly. I said "murder", not assassination. I therefore think at this moment, that this killer, if he is not shot dead by the police, will rather quickly be free. If he could therefore leave my country and commit his atrocities elsewhere, that would suit me well. It is only for this reason that it seems sensible for me to let him know that he would be welcome in an Islamic army to kill the military enemy, that is to say, in the current context, British, French and American soldiers.

He looks genuinely interested while continuing to fidget a little, to look everywhere around him while listening to me. Is he looking for the police? Is he careful not to be attacked? Is he uncomfortable with these curious people staring at him? Or is he eager to get it over with? This last thought seems to me to be the fairest because it is the most logical: He can only be eager to see all this end. I would like him to talk to me more, to share his thoughts. Unfortunately, he is not very expansive despite my efforts.

Regardless, he gives me his opinion on what I have just mentioned.

I too would like to see the end of it. It is not so much because of the situation, but the fact of not knowing for how much longer I have to stay there (because there is no way for me to let him go before the forces, whoever they are, have the situation and the killers in hand); for not knowing what is happening "on the other side", on the police side; and what I should do: stay or go because they might want to see me somewhere else. This is my anxious side.

Everything is too calm, I do not think help has arrived.

All of a sudden, he gets excited. He mutters disgruntled: "Shitty recording camera," and walks away. He goes to the other side of the street. I don't try to hold him back firstly because the suddenness of his departure stunned me and by the time I come back from being surprised, he is already far away; secondly because he wants to stop a recording, not commit another murder. So if the person filming us knows what is good for them, they will not dispute stopping their activity. Otherwise, I do not think it will go any further than a phone being thrown down to smash it or a slap in the face. I "feel" that nothing more serious than that will happen. I hope so. I pray.

(A small thought that has been going round my head since the beginning of writing this book: it is insane how long it takes to write or say what I thought at the time in a flash of a second).

Eighth minute

I take advantage of this moment to go and see the other one, his accomplice. He is now standing in front of the hood of the wrecked car. Seeing me walking towards him, he comes to meet me.

I ask him:
"How do you feel?"

No answer.

"How are you?"

Still no response.

"You don't look like you've done much," and in my head I finish the sentence: "in this murder". Deliberately, I refuse to use the words: knife, weapon, accident, murder, and the like.

He is still not reacting.

He is tall, less handsome and younger than the killer. He looks clumsy and not very lively, not very smart either and seems very shy. Also with his beard, he looks more like an Islamist than his accomplice. He holds in his left hand the large clean knife of his accomplice. His hands too are clean, which makes me think that he did not touch the injured body of the young man.

My hands are still in the pockets of my sleeveless jacket. They have not come out.

I ask him if he would like to give me "this" looking at the knife and holding out a hand. He looks at me as if he does not understand what I am saying and does not answer me. I repeat my request; this time he shakes his head no.

I am still trying to strike up a conversation:
"What will you do next?"

He only responds with a negative shake of the head.

I insist:
"Nothing planned? Are you just waiting for the police to arrive?"

A big blank; not a sound comes out of his mouth. He looks embarrassed, like he has never spoken to a woman.

I then propose to him the following thing to try to shock him and therefore, to force him to react:
"Why won't you run away?"

Despite the objective of this proposal, I cannot believe what I have just said. If he really leaves, I will look smart! What justification or excuse could I give to the police if they learn that one of the killers left, right after I spoke to him? At the same time, if he only witnessed the murder at the express request of the other one without having hurt this young man in any way, does he deserve to be arrested? Prison, in the sense of rubbing shoulders with hardened criminals, will no doubt only have a detrimental effect on him. But he just shakes his head. Again to say no. So, I tell him about the intentions of his accomplice, namely to be killed by the police. I told him it would be a shame if he got shot too. Therefore, he has to go.

When I talk to him, I leave a time between each sentence. Like with the other killer, I do not want to rush him either. I watch for his reactions but he has none. Watching him walk, move, express himself, I wonder how he could have killed this young man in such a violent way; where he worked up the nervous courage to run into him with the car and stab him in the body. Obviously, he did nothing. He does not seem capable of it. After all, he still saw everything: he must have been in the car, on the passenger side. If I had been there, I would have been filled with adrenaline and I would be shaking from head to toe. My heart would be pounding. Even ten minutes after the accident. From him, nothing. Otherwise he is an extraordinary actor who possesses no less extraordinary self-control. But I do not think so. I am more and more convinced that he was manipulated by the other one and that his contribution to the development of the plan of the murder and then to its realisation is more than minimal. To be shot for having been present and obedient is a dear price to pay.

So, I offer him once again to leave, to go away, to go home for instance. Of course it is not up to me to decide whether he is guilty or not and to judge his action or non-action. But, he looks so lost... And even if the world will not miss him, I cannot bring myself to see him killed just because his accomplice decided to. Given his lack of strength of character, perhaps he could not find enough willpower in himself to refuse to accompany him and then to accept to be shot down by the police. Unless, in order to become someone, he chose to copy the other one. I tell myself that the detectives will not have too much trouble finding him and arresting him.
He shakes his head again, meaning no.

Suddenly, I prick up my ears: emergency sirens. I hear sirens again in the distance. Spaced sounds that stop quickly. It is starting to move.

Ninth minute

I decide to speak to him more firmly in my choice of words:
"Leave, I said to him, go! Leave before the police arrive. I don't think you want to get killed, so get out while there's still time."

He looks at me terrified and for the first time, utters a word, in a low voice:

"No, no" he said while shaking a hand.

I have the feeling of having in front of me a fifteen-year-old teenager to whom I have just proposed to dance a slow dance. He has that same expression of childish terror on his face.
Considering that he is in no way dangerous and not wanting to leave the killer alone any longer, I decide not to linger with this one and turn to the other one.

As I leave, a small, yellow vehicle emerges to the right side of the white truck. What makes me think it is an ambulance? Is it written on it or just the look of the vehicle? I should be happy to see it because it finally arrived. This poor young man is finally going to be rescued. On the contrary, I am worried because this car is so small that it could not even carry a medium-sized dog in a lying position. I examine this vehicle which rolls gently in our direction to find other clues which can certify to me that it is indeed an ambulance: it is so small. I did not even know that it existed.

I try to reassure myself by telling me that this may be a first dispatch in charge of giving first aid to the victims, and that the paramedics will decide later if a larger ambulance is necessary to transport the victim to the hospital or not.

The small ambulance slows down again and I see the driver watching the scene and the victim. I tell myself that he is looking for the best place to park. But to my amazement, the vehicle picks up speed and drive off. It is surreal! An ambulance that does not take care of an injured person! I have never seen that. What is happening? I am stunned. For a second, the image of that woman knocked down on a French motorway that no one wanted to help came back to me.

In the seventies, summer holidays were very important for the French. Not working for thirty days. What a jubilation! There were the Julyists (those leaving in July) and the Augustians (those leaving in August). They set off for the sun and the sea, resolving to spend their thirty days of holidays there: the better-off had their second home; the less wealthy went to the campsite, often the same one from year to year. As planes were still expensive and tourism infrastructure underdeveloped, people rarely went abroad. They still loved their country and they enjoyed visiting it.

In order not to lose a single day of holidays, the car was loaded on Friday evening, just after the last hour of work, and on Saturday morning, the French were on the roads in the direction of their holiday spot, creating monster traffic jams and many accidents. That year, I must have been eight or nine years old. In the car driven by my father and which was taking us to La Vendée, there was my step-mother (my father's second wife) and my two sisters. My parents had divorced two or three years earlier and my two sisters and I spent every other weekend and half of the school holidays with our father.

My father had bought a small house in Olonne-sur-Mer to offer us holidays at the sea side and it was where we were going to. The motorway was loaded, cars bumper to bumper. As soon as it moved a little, cars abruptly accelerated. Along the motorway were hitchhikers (in the seventies, the French paid little attention to the Highway code, and used the roads as they pleased, killing an average of fifteen thousand of them every year on the roads of France. Today, with the help of fines, they have become more disciplined).

One of them, a rather chubby young girl in shorts and a shirt with a backpack, had had the bad idea of standing in the middle of the motorway, certainly with the intention of getting a lift more easily. Suddenly, a few cars were moving fast and one of them struck the girl. I saw her fly high and fall heavily, landing with her legs bent, her feet turned outward, her knees inward. When we approached, I saw that she was unable to move: she sat there in shock like a body without legs. I begged my father to stop and pick her up to take her to the hospital. He refused, saying we didn't have time. Turning around, I looked out through the back windshield to see if anyone would take pity on this young girl. The motorway being in a straight line, I could see it for a long time. But no car stopped. I was shocked. Shocked to see that the driver of the car that had hit her, had got no decency towards her; that all the cars passed by her without anyone to help her; that my dad "didn't have time". As if you had to have time to help someone in distress! How ugly humanity was!

At six years old, I had discovered perfidy and had become a mythomaniac, taking refuge in the animal world.

That day, I discovered selfishness. And it was in this world that I had to live, to exist! No thanks. This total lack of compassion for a wounded human being had cut my will to live. From this incident and in spite of myself, since I had to live, I was going to become slowly but surely more unmanageable, more difficult.

In the distance, I hear more and more sirens. A siren sounds; it quickly stops and does not come closer. Then another sounded for a few seconds, still in the distance, then was no longer heard. And a third, a fourth, and so on. But why are there so many emergency vehicles in the distance? Could there be another more serious accident, which would explain why help is still not there?

Tenth minute

It is time to go back to HIM. I hear him shout but I only catch the last words: "Piss off!" and I see the Caribbean mother and daughter walking away. It is just unbelievable! The daughter took advantage of my absence to fetch her mother. Then, they both went to talk to the killer. But what did they say to him in the space of twenty or thirty seconds to annoy him? When I had left him, he was irritated, chasing the prying people who had come too close in order to record us; now it is the Caribbean girl who pisses him off.   I tell myself all my work to calm him down is wasted. What will happen now?

Caribbean mother and daughter leave. The injured young man is now alone. He still continues to bleed. I had thought that maybe the mother's caress had caused the blood to circulate, explaining why the victim was bleeding. But it is clear that he bleeds alone, without help. I am now certain that his heart is beating. It is comforting to know that he is in a coma because he is not in pain that way. Since no one intends to rescue him, all that is left for him to do is to die quickly.

Now that I have turned around (the round trip to the other killer), I dare to look at the other part of the street. I have a shock: it is crowded with people. Not for a second have I thought that so many people have stopped by: they are so silent. There are dozens and dozens of them on the pavements, some perched on parked cars and on the wall that runs from the gate to the boulevard. Others even posted themselves quite close to the damaged car and therefore to the two killers. I even had to push one away. But what can interest them? What are they waiting for? What are they hoping to see? Do they not have anything better to do with their day?

I see the killer walking towards me, calmly. It is reassuring. The Caribbean girl had pissed him off, but he comes looking for my company, probably because I am interested in him. So he thinks of nothing else. For the moment.

On the unhealthy curious side, the situation worsens: the neighbourhood nursery school has just finished and the mothers who came to collect their children find nothing better to do than to approach the place of the accident. The herd is growing rapidly.

Then, they stop to revel in the spectacle before them: a car half-pressed in a lamppost, a man and a woman talking to each other, another man standing in front of the hood of the wrecked car and a man on the ground, partly covered with his jacket and bleeding. Their children are standing in front of them. None of them speak. They stay there, without moving. Arriving from the perpendicular street, they find themselves on the side of the white truck, quite close to the victim and the car. They expose their three or four year old children to a wounded and bleeding man. What the hell are they thinking? Is this a sight for a toddler? But the worst is that it is easy to see the weapons these men carry, especially the killer's. At any moment, one of these children can escape from their mother's arms and come towards us, towards the injured person, to touch him perhaps, or even towards the killer, curious to see more closely the "shiny things". What will his reaction be? I mentally prepare myself to intervene.

In any case, if the killer has a sudden desire to repeat what he did, potential victims are aplenty. But what are the rescuers doing? Where have they gone? We would be in a small village in the middle of fields that it would not take them longer to show up.

Not wanting to awaken his murderous instincts for revenge and above all, not wanting him to turn his head towards the children, in the hope that he would spot them as late as possible, I change the subject. I tell him about the British army "which, in general, in countries at war where they are deployed, have a role of guardian of peace and order, not of war. The soldiers patrol, ensuring the security of the civilians. They distribute food and medicine. And very often, they make friends with the population, playing with the children. But, they do not fight and above all, they do not kill civilians. Their role is neutral, their presence reassuring, unlike the American army, which is an ideological army. When they deploy in a country, it is often with the aim of making it an American-style democracy without the consent of the population or local government."

From time to time, he repeats a word or two. Since I do not dare to look at him too often in the eyes, I cannot tell if he is listening to me, attentively or not, or if he is somewhere else.

I am on the impression that he too is listening to what is happening in the distance. He also heard the sirens. Does he wonder what the rescuers are doing? What did he think when he saw the ambulance driving away?

As far as he is concerned, it has been more than ten minutes, almost fifteen, since he crushed this young man. And nothing! Neither the police nor the fire brigade nor the ambulances seem to be interested in his little revenge.

I have the feeling of being in another world, a world where one comes to look very closely at a seriously injured man lying on the ground and an assassin with bloody hands, without any embarrassment; a world where young girls walk fearlessly past killers to pick up their mothers to go shopping; a world where ambulances do not stop to treat the injured and carry away the dead; a world where mothers drag their children to the scene of an accident and watch the victims bleed with as much detachment as if they were taking them to the park or the circus; a world where rescuers of all kinds do not come to the aid of people and vehicles involved in an accident; a world where killers speak excellent language without any swear words of any kind. It is "la la land", the kingdom of the absurd where nothing is as it should be; nothing happens as it should, following the established rules of our society. A screenwriter or a novelist would have written it in a story, he would have been accused of smoking hard drugs so it is unlikely. It is said that reality often exceeds fiction; there, the excess is so titanic that it makes fiction impossible.

In the distance, there are no longer any sirens. It is silence.

Eleventh minute

I end it "by suggesting to him that in the future, if he wants to kill a soldier, he should set his sight on an American one". I have nothing against the Americans but I prefer the English, more courteous and more respectful. He listens to me, seems interested, and does not respond to my proposal.

And now, I don't know what to say to him. I am starting to feel tired.

Suddenly, an idea occurs to me. What if the sirens heard in the distance were actually for us? I imagine the police wanting to approach discreetly so as not to frighten the killers. They put on their emergency siren to circulate in London and two hundred yards from here, stop them. Vehicle after vehicle. Then they post themselves at various strategic places in order to have a good overview of the murder scene and the two killers.

Inspired by cinematic memories, I watch the rooftops of surrounding houses for snipers posted up there, ready to shoot the assassins. After all, they are both armed, although a knife is less dangerous than a gun in the sense that it can only kill a close body, no further than an arm's length away. However, if someone has reported this to the police, I imagine they must take a thousand precautions before approaching to arrest them. My presence and that of the Caribbean lady should have inclined them to think that the danger was not so great. But even the paramedic did not stop to treat the victim.

In fact, it is quite serious because medical vehicles have always been considered neutral and harmless. At war, on a battlefield, the stretcher-bearers dressed in white who come to pick up the wounded are never shot. Generally, an ambulance or the ambulance crews are never attacked. It is a global consensus respected by all. The fact that this little yellow ambulance did not stop is a bad sign. How could the paramedic feel more in danger here than in a country at war? So what about the police? It is certain that they are more often assaulted than the paramedics. Is that why they are still not here? Are they afraid? Are they overly protecting themselves? Or are they preparing for a successful arrest?

Without any more clues than those sirens heard in the distance and my power of deduction, I tell myself that law enforcement is finally about. I continue to scan the crowd around me for a uniform, any service car and the roofs looking for the silhouette of a man but I do not see anything. How to know for sure? I need to know because if they are here, my presence can only hinder them: they will not dare to intervene for fear of putting me in danger nor shoot for fear of hitting me. But if I am mistaken, if they are not present nearby, I cannot leave HIM, abandon all three of them. God knows what would happen then, especially what would be H reaction. Personally, I am ready to stay as long as necessary. But how do you know when the "necessary" ceases to be? What clue will tell me when to leave, that the situation is in the hands of law enforcement ready to take control? I pray they think about it and send me a sign, whatever it is.

How difficult and dizzying it is to imagine a situation, to deduce a fact from such a slight clue. I cannot believe myself; I do not trust myself. Still, it makes sense. There can be no other explanation. Anyhow, the police will have to arrive even if they are scared out of their mind. They will have to solve this problem, take away this injured young man, surely dead now. They will have to inform his family and arrest his murderers. It cannot go on forever. I have to stop looking around. I am afraid my worry will reach the killer.

I do not remember exactly what I said to him, nor how I came to say it to him, but I do remember talking to him about America and its president. A thought in passing. And that interested him. So much the better!

Without my realising it, while I was talking to him, he took several steps and I followed him. He did not walk, only took two steps here, three steps there. I notice that we are now quite a distance away from the injured young man. Is he looking for something? Or is he just anxious? In fact, during these ten minutes spent with him, he did not stop moving.

While speaking to him, I continue to think because I have to conclude my thought. I have to take a stand in order to handle the situation. I choose to take the most logical course, to believe that they are here and I become a little less anxious (nothing serious, I am easily anxious). Of course they are here round the corner, quite close to us and invisible.

From now on, I have to treat it as a team effort: the police (or similar service) and me. While I keep the killer occupied, while I divert his attention, they take the time to deploy themselves, to position themselves at the best strategic points for a successful arrest, without killing or being killed and without any blunder. I just have to wait for the signal that will let me know when to leave the place. I am certain the police think I am smart enough to understand. On the other hand, I am much less sure that they appreciate my intervention. They generally do not like to share the tasks and owe part of the success of their mission to a civilian or even to another service. We will see about that later: I intend, if I have the possibility, to ask them the question. Just to know. And spare the susceptibilities if the situation should ever arise again.

And if I did something wrong, I also would like to know, to correct myself. I am not afraid of being wrong because it allows me to learn, to know and not to repeat my stupidity in order to not upset anyone. I do not think the perfect little manual on "How to Talk to a Killer and Engage His Attention" exists but someone in some ministerial department must have laid down a regulation of recommendations on how to do it safely for yourself, one of the many chapters of the sacred book of the British government: "Whatever You Want to Do, Never Forget to Make Yourself a Very Thick Shell of Cotton Wool Beforehand to Avoid the Slightest Little Boo that this Rascal of Life Likes to Get in Your Way. Here is How"!

So I wait and I resume my reflection on the United States and its president. *(Was it because I was thinking too much about something else that made me forget what I said to him?*

Twelfth minute

So, it is said, they are here: the MET Police (the London police), the MPSFC (Metropolitan Police Specialist Firearms Command), Scotland Yard, the militaries, whatever... They had enough time to repatriate to London half of the military and civilian forces of England. I do not hear anything, I do not see anything but I think they are present, posted not far away. I was starting to feel de-energised, flat; this thought invigorates me.

Now I have to spot and understand the sign they will send to let me know that I have to leave.

The two killers also begin to feel something. They fidget more; they have become closer to each other and speak to one another more and more often, short exchanges. The killer goes back and forth between his accomplice and me.

The crowd does not flinch, does not move: they continue to feast their eyes on the "spectacle".

As for me, I tell myself that this is the most critical moment. If the police are around, they also brought cameras with them to film everything. That is what we are told in detective films and TV series: to record everything in the event of a complaint or a blunder. There is no reason for the killer to think otherwise.

This is therefore the perfect opportunity for him to put on a show: What could be better than killing another person to show what he is still capable of or even molesting a child to become a monster in the eyes of all and therefore have maximum publicity since it is about revenge. Vengeance generally has two purposes: to return the evil and to make it known.

More than ever, I am on my guard.

I check that the mothers and their children have not come forward, hoping that they have left, the child having grown impatient for example. Bad luck, the pairs are still there. In the same place.
I also watch the crowd. It sometimes happens that a coward, to make everyone believe that he is very brave but knowing that he will only do it for a few seconds, starts to attack the killers.

Then, for some reason, the idea that this murder is a settling of accounts between gangs, something local and not at all religious crosses my mind. Like in the movie "The Wild One" with Marlon Brando. After all, wanting to do battle with the police is a badge of honour within these gangs; and making the front page of local newspapers, a way of letting everyone know that "I am an almighty leader, please don't step on my toes again or you know what to expect".
And evidently, in these times of terror, nothing is better than talking about Allah and revenge against a background of Islam to get the whole world interested in you.

The Qur'an is a book of love that speaks of respect and peace for everyone and there are madmen who use it as an excuse to kill and sow terror. They would better read it first. They would learn a thing or two about the peace professed by their prophet Muhammad, a very wise man. And it is so good and much easier to live in peace.

My killer calls himself a Muslim. Not only does he not wear a beard, but he has nothing against women. He is a Muslim terrorist beyond category. Or else he is not. Of course, to me, it is becoming obvious, it is gang related. That is why I do not believe him. But then, if he is part of a gang, the other members of this gang may want to intervene to prevent the arrest of the two killers. I watch the crowd for the slightest movement or signs between them. Nothing.
All the same, for a gang leader, he is very polite and his language is too chastised. Same if he is a terrorist. It is hard to understand him. Nothing is obvious.

I am starting to wonder how to announce him that I leave.

Something tells me it will not be long now.

The accomplice is now as close to me as the killer. They seem to have, by an unspoken mutual agreement, decided to stay together. Why had they separated at the start, one staying next to the victim and the car, and the other one a hundred yards away?

During the time spent with them, I took care to always leave at least a yard of space, that is to say, the length of an arm and a little more between them and me. So they could not grab me, slap me, kick me, or stab me. In theory.

Now, I have the feeling that we are coming out of a semi torpor and that something is going to change. Nothing lets me predict it if not the time already elapsed; it is rather a sensation, something indefinable. From time to time, we look at each other, looking to one another for an answer, a clue.

At this point, I do not know what to say to him to divert his attention. Besides, he is nearer to his accomplice than to me now and as I do not want to get too close to them, he comes back to me regularly but does not stay.

The crowd of onlookers gets a little louder. Something is happening.

I turn around and see a woman walking towards us in the middle of the street without hurrying. When she is closer to me, I seem to recognise the woman who had come at the beginning of my intervention to examine the victim and the killer. What does she want now? I step back a little to let her pass between the killer and me, thinking she is going to look at the victim again. In fact, she is heading towards me. In a low voice, she asks me:

"Are you going to leave soon?"

I ask her:
"What for? Are you from the police?

"No," she tells me.

"Then I stay. No question of leaving him alone until the police are there."

Then still in a low voice, she asks me a second question:
"Do you know his intentions?"

"Yes," I answer her. "He wants to attack the police and get shot."

Having satisfied her curiosity, she goes back as she came, calmly. Decidedly, I will never get used to it. But what does it matter to her what he intends to do! I look at the killer to see his reaction. Not much. He seems slightly satisfied that he is taken care of. Although I do not think he heard our little conversation, he must suspect it is about him. I grumble against this woman who definitely has not an ounce of embarrassment.

Thirteenth minute

But all of a sudden, I am enlightened. She is the sign I am waiting for. This woman is a Police "spy", sent to fish for information. Sending a woman makes sense since the killer tolerates them around him. Maybe she is an undercover policewoman herself. And for fear that he could hear us despite her precautions, she could not admit that the police were there or that she herself was one of them. Yet, if true, that would mean the police have been there all along. I cannot believe that. It is quite strange!

Without any other more specific and logical clue, I decide that this is the expected signal to leave the scene. But it is out of question to leave him like that, especially just after this woman. It would seem suspicious to him. So I wait a bit. I "keep busy" by looking at the crowd, looking for the police or other armed forces. Then I look at Them with an air of saying: "Everything is fine".

More seriously, I keep watching around me looking for an excuse to leave him. Even if I leave time between the woman and me so as not to seem I am leaving because she spoke to me, he is intelligent and he will make the connection. So I need a very different reason.

God hears me and I see my bus backing up. I look at the killer, I show him my bus, and I tell him that "the bus being ready to leave, I have to go. All my luggage is inside, I cannot miss it". I ask him if he is okay with me leaving. He replies yes. I ask him if I can do something for him, he says no. Finally I ask him if he needs anything. He says no again. In the movies, the outlaws who did not manage to escape on time or who thought they could defy the police and then, at the last minute, change their minds, always ask for money and a car to get away, escape. So I do almost the same and I ask him if he wants a car. No is still his answer. So I conclude by saying:

"Well I'm leaving." He does not answer.

These are the last words I address him. I do not say goodbye to him, the same way I did not say hello nor ask for his name because my intervention was in no way a social conversation. Having had my back to the bus, I turn around and, walking neither fast nor slow, I head for the 53.

The driver, who had closed the door behind me after I had left the bus, seeing me arrive, opens it.
I go back to my place and I note with satisfaction that no one has touched my luggage, not even my handbag.

I have not been sitting for ten or fifteen seconds when a man gets on the bus and shouts, "Get down! Get down!". Everyone obeys. I, curious as a cat, look out the window. Luckily, I am sitting on the right side of the bus. I am therefore able to see a police car arriving quickly and stopping in front of the bus. Then, two doors open and a policeman and a policewoman come out, pointing a gun in front of them.

Meanwhile, the two killers started running, the one I spoke to in the direction of the police, threatening and brandishing his weapon; the other one, his accomplice in the opposite direction, towards the boulevard. Then two quiet noises are heard. I do not immediately understand that these are gunshots because the noise that the revolvers have just made has nothing to do with the noise you hear in detective films. Warned that he wanted to be shot down, the police shoot them in the legs. I see them both crumble. The second gets up and tries again to run away; he takes another bullet. Then the scene of the murder is invaded by men in uniform who rush in on the two killers on the ground. I do not see anyone going to the victim.

Out of the blue, everyone starts screaming on the bus. I shout, "Calm down, calm down. Listen, it's all over. Calm down" for almost a minute, until quietness returns. Passengers have to calm down because I do not want a panic-driven stampede down the narrow little stairway that leads to the top floor of the bus.

I also see mothers hugging their child or baby so tightly that they nearly suffocate them. There were no more deaths at the crime scene; I do not want any on the bus.

Then a police officer enters the vehicle to let us know that we can leave. I walk over to him and ask him if he wants my ID and statement as a witness because I have been with the killers for almost fifteen minutes. He replies that it is not necessary. I then ask him to confirm that I can freely leave, which he validates. It is over!

Afterwards

1)

I will not see the rest of the police operation because my bus is backing up to the boulevard. Then it turns right to resume its journey via another route. I naively think it is still going to Parliament Square, Westminster, where is its final stop. Unfortunately, it only goes to Lewisham where they make us to take another bus. It bothers me terribly. I have to transfer all my luggage from one bus to another. Worse still, this new bus is not going to Westminster, I will have to change buses again. I am now more than half an hour late. So I send a text message to my children to reassure them. Well, maybe reassuring is not the right word since I tell them about a shooting on the road as the reason for my delay. The texts being short, I cannot develop. The truth comes to them raw, enough to puzzle them while waiting for me to arrive, if I ever get there, that is!

I finally arrive at the pub where I have a rendezvous with my children. Without even greeting his mother, my son asks me:
"A shooting? What do you mean by a shooting?"
So I tell them everything that just happened, insisting more on a settling of scores between gangs than Islamic terror.

My son is not too pleased:
"Mum, you could have been killed, you could have been injured!"

"No my darling," I answer him, "I was in no danger."

My daughter doesn't say anything, her way to react when she is shocked or scared.

I still have time before my bus leaves. So we order some food. The journey is long, I need dinner before leaving even if it is not very late in the afternoon. Then, my children accompany me to Victoria station where I take the coach that will take me to Cornwall.

When kissing them goodbye, I ask them to keep an eye on the news so they can tell me what really happened in Woolwich and who these two guys are.

I advise them to listen to the local news, which will only talk about what happens in London on the day, thinking that the national press could not be interested in this little news item.

Sitting in the coach, I get prepared for a ten-hour trip. I put on some music that I listen to with headphones and I take out my book.

About twenty minutes later, my son calls me to tell me that on television, the murder of the young man is breaking news. It is the only items of news on all the television channels. They said these guys are terrorists. I thank him for the information which surprises me and I hang up. What must they be talking about?

Five minutes later, my son calls me back to tell me that there is a photo of me talking with one of the killers on the Internet and that it is weird seeing me there.

Three minutes did not pass that he calls me back to tell me this time, that the photo is now on television and they ask if anyone knows the woman who is talking to the terrorist. On the Internet too, her name is requested. So, he calls to ask me if I would accept him to disclose my name. I agree.

Barely five minutes passed when he calls me again to tell me this time that a journalist has contacted him about interviewing the woman in the photo. So would I be okay with him giving the journalist my mobile phone number? Once more, I accepted thinking this journalist works for a London magazine or newspaper.

Indeed, my phone rings shortly after and it is a reporter from the Evening Standard who would like to interview me. Not wanting the whole coach to hear me, I duck down head to my feet, still sitting in my seat, to talk to him.

As soon as I hang up, my phone rings again. Never have I been called so many times in such a short period of time I thought, while putting my book in my bag. It is another journalist who, too, wants to interview me.

In fact, and in short, I spent eight hours bent over talking to my feet and to a good two dozen journalists, telling them all the same story over and over again.

It is now about one o'clock in the morning. I have just hung up and once again, the mobile rings. This time, it is to the television channel ITV that I answer. With them, it is shorter. After telling me that they tried all evening to get hold of me, the young woman asks me where I am. Having no idea, I ask the driver who answers me:
"We will be in Plymouth in ten minutes."

I repeat it to the person on the phone who tells me:
"Get off at Plymouth, I'll send you a taxi back to London."

I cannot believe it. I almost made it home! I am tired; my arms hurt from carrying all my luggage and my foot aches; and now I have to go back to London. So I get off and shortly after, a car arrives.

The driver is nice and we talk for a while. Then I apologise because I would like to get some sleep. I will not arrive in London until four in the morning, and even though ITV has been kind enough to book me a room in a great hotel, I will not have time to enjoy it because they plan for me to appear in a show that starts at seven o'clock.

Indeed, it is after four o'clock when I enter the room. I decide not to sleep because it is more tiring to sleep for two hours than not to sleep at all. So I opt for a good bath and a big breakfast because I am starving.

In the ITV studios, the video that the killer forced a passer-by to record on his smartphone (which will be explained to me later) is playing on loop on all their screens and is subtitled "Terrorist Attack". I see this black man with entirely red hands, shouting something that I do not understand. He talks like those extremists, with anger. It is HIM but I do not recognise him. He looks so different: his look, his tone, his facial expression are not what I saw and heard for thirteen minutes. His hands are also different. In front of me, they were only soiled with a little blood. In this video, they are bright red.

I dare not ask who he is. I am trying to remember a detail of clothing to help me identify him. It is embarrassing because I was invited to speak about my intervention and I do not recognise on this video the one with whom I spoke.

Above all, I have to process the fact that he and his accomplice are terrorists. As far as I am concerned, a terrorist is someone who puts bombs in public places and kills several people. They did not do that. But as my son says: "They may have killed only one person and with a car and a knife but they wanted to sow terror. So they are terrorists".

For the next two days, it is non-stop interview after interview: in various hotels, in television studios, in radio studios... I am made up, I have my hair done, I am pampered. I discover a whole new world that I did not know. The meals eaten in the restaurant are excellent; some encounters are magical. My last interview on the second day is for the BBC. We have to take the train to the BBC West Country studio. Then I am put on the train and I can finally go home. It is ten o'clock in the evening when I open my door.

2)

For six months, I give interviews almost daily, and the following six months, weekly.

I am invited to go to Germany for a show.

I receive various and varied awards, which give me the opportunity to meet great people and have fun. Every award I scoop moves me because it shows how much my action has affected the British people. The most surprising prize, and the one that perhaps touched me the most, is the GG2 Leadership Award. It was surprising because it is an award given by the Asian Media and Marketing Group to Asians, that is, to Indians (from India). Which I am not. I married an Iranian and I am very popular in South Korea which makes me Asian in heart but certainly not in blood or culture. However, this Indian group decided that I was worth one of them and elected me for this award. So it moved me to be "adopted".

I was even honoured with the Medal of Courage by the French government. My children and I were invited to the 14th of July Garden Party at the French Embassy for the occasion. And during the reception, Mr. Ambassador pinned the medal on my jacket. I had never hoped to be awarded a medal as were all my ascendants; since we no longer live at war, there is, for a civilian, no longer any opportunity to "earn" one.

On the other hand, and despite all the requests for medals made by the people of Great Britain, I got nothing from the English government. Not even the civic medal from my town. Yet my English family has done as much for the greatness of the United Kingdom as my French family has done for that of France. As the saying goes: "No-one is a prophet in his own land".

Never mind!

3)

That is the good side of things. Unfortunately, it is very light compared to the other side of the coin.

To start with, I had the police on my back. For three years, the MET, the London police have been tormenting me. As soon as one of them saw me on the street, he walked towards me, start asking me useless questions, grab my wrists with force, twist my arms and harass me more and more as my anxiety attacks increased. And for at least half an hour. Then he let me call my son. From then, I would only use the back streets to avoid them.

Once they even took me to a police station, in the middle of the night, for no reason other than for fun, and put me in the cell, while leaving the door open, tortured my arms and laughed at me. I got so sick with anxiety I asked to see a doctor, they refused.

Each time I had to call my son for help. He is the one who always ended up calming them down on the phone before coming to get me. They were really horrible.

At home, the situation has deteriorated. I pass on the fact, not very important compared to what I endure on a daily basis, that the mayor of my city completely ignored me.

The children and teenagers who tormented me, who verbally abused me, physically attacked and damaged my house since I moved to Helston, continued to do so but with all the more violence because they now know my name and use it to personalise their verbal harassment. In South West Cornwall, when children and teenagers scream and scream, damage nature and urban material, attack people verbally and physically, it is called "playing". They are therefore never reprimanded nor even educated, that is to say explained to them respect for others and things. So the police never arrest anyone, not even adults who do the same. South West Cornwall is a lawless wild land. Life there is very difficult.

For a few months, I also had part of the black population on my back. While some verbally abused me, others tried to calm them down. It was very weird.

I do not understand why some people absolutely want to be famous. I found the position quite negative because it puts you in a weak position. It is no longer possible to say something without it being reported and above all distorted and it has become impossible for me to defend myself. After having been praised, some newspapers tried to tear the heroin down. What for? The Daily Mail even accused me of being racist and having been sectioned. Without any proof to buttress their accusations. Unfortunately, three other newspapers, including a local one, took up this damaging news. The Daily Mail even went so far as to publish this slanderous article three times in the space of six months and leave it permanently on their Mail Online site. What is the point of this kind of article? They didn't sell more newspapers than usual with this lying piece of paper. I am not sure that the English people want their heroin to be portrayed as a racist and a crazy piece of trash. On the other hand, the consequences were serious for me: this horror of tabloid ruined my life, because a professor or a teacher in England must be cleaner than clean; they teach children and young persons, they must be blameless to get hired. Consequently, I have been unemployed since 2013. I wanted to sue them, which a lot of famous people do because the Daily Mail is a defamatory rag, but I couldn't find any lawyer brave enough to do it for me, nor a court to judge the case.

There was also this little case that my insurance brought to court because I refused the 50/50 that the insurance offered me. The other male driver had left his parking space without looking where he was backing up and bumped into my car as I had just pulled into the parking lot and was driving down the main driveway. The driver was a middle-aged man and his description was part of the report along with the damage to the car. However, in court, it was an old man who claimed to be the driver.

When I told the lady Judge of Truro that it was not him, and that the proof is in the declarations made to the insurance since I described the driver to the company, she looked at me as if to say "Don't take advantage of your fame to get anything" and asked me, "Is it that important?" I was so flabbergasted at her response that I did not know what to say. So she decided to continue the hearing. It is obvious that she could only return a verdict of "not guilty for failure to drive with due care and attention" since he was not the right driver. I could not do anything because I was famous. I found it sickeningly unfair.

A pharmacist of African descent tried to poison me with the wrong medicine. The more I told him it was the wrong medicine, the more he insisted that it was the right one and that I had to take it. Then, to prevent me from filing a complaint against him, which was not my intention, he, forty-eight hours later, filed a complaint for racism against me. I was able to demonstrate to the police the falsity of this statement. Then the police refused to take my complaint against him for his defamatory accusation on the pretext that he was black and that I was famous.

I could say so much more. For three years, it was hell. I do not understand why people want to be famous. It is terribly difficult to live because those who do not love you are jealous of you and therefore lead you a hellish life. They are unfortunately much more numerous than those who admire you. In my case anyway. It is not having confronted killers that gave me post-traumatic stress disorder but rather this situation of daily harassment and of having received no help from any authority whatsoever.

To add yet another element to the realm of the absurd, the terrorist I spoke to was more polite, better educated, and has been more respectful to me than the vast majority of my townspeople and the police: A Scotland Yard detective came to take my statement at a secret house somewhere in Cornwall. I then asked her several questions that bothered me. She refused to answer them before the end of the investigation and the court judgment, promising me to do so afterwards. She gave me her business card with her phone number asking me to call her when it was all over and she would answer all my questions. I called her several times but she never wanted to talk to me; so I have no response to date.

Even ITV, to which I gave a lot of time, jumped on board by refusing to give me the "Pride of Britain" trophy which the British people had voted for me in very large numbers. Literally, at the last second, as the show was about to start taping, and I was there in the studios with my kids and the other winners, all dressed up, ITV asked us to leave. A man explained to me that some judge had asked him for the case not to be mentioned before the judgment. ITV could very well have done the ceremony, then cut my appearance in the edit to broadcast it later since the ceremony was not live. This man did not want to hear anything. My children and I were devastated. He promised us that we would be invited again the following year in order to collect the prize. They even wrote me a letter to reiterate their intention. But, that never happened. ITV never wanted to give me the award.

I was therefore unable to thank all those who had voted for me but also all those who wrote to me at home without knowing my address (Bravo to the post office which was able to deliver all these letters simply labelled "Angel of Woolwich. Helston Cornwall). I therefore take advantage of this book to do it so. I was very touched by all your little words written in pretty cards or simply on a piece of paper as well as by all the messages on Facebook or Messenger. Between the interviews and the number of messages received, it has been impossible for me to answer you all. Once again, thank you very much from the bottom of my heart. Your messages have sincerely touched me.

Epilogue

I, as always, wanted to help an injured person. It had always gone well. This time the driver turned out to be an Islamic killer and a terrorist and the whole planet talked about it. It brought me a lot of trouble and stress. So, yes, for a moment, I regretted having intervened. But I know myself, I am incapable of not helping someone in difficulty, whoever it is, if I have the ability to help or support morally.

Because despite all the troubles that certain situations can bring, I believe that a little kindness can go far in the heart and/or positively impact the future of the person who receives it.

Thank you

I would like to thank my two children Pawony and Basil as well as their father, Behrouz for their help in proofreading the manuscript and their contribution on various small things,
with a more emphatic thank you for Pawony who proofread the English version of the book and who took care of the "sensitive" side of the language;
and for Basil who designed the cover of the book with great skill.

And finally, a big thank you to all my friends for their friendship and support.

Printed in Poland
by Amazon Fulfillment
Poland Sp. z o.o., Wrocław

19853212R00047